## ABOUT THE AUTHOR

**Asma Elbadawi** is a British Sudanese born in Sudan and raised in England Sports Inclusivity Consultant, Basketball Player and Spoken Word Poet. Elbadawi holds a BA Hons in Photography, Video and Digital Imaging and a Masters in Visual Arts. Her dual cultural heritage deeply influences her creativity with her main focus being female empowerment. She is best known for her involvement in the globally successful FIBA ALLOW HIJAB Campaign. This campaign saw the International Basketball Federation FIBA allow Muslim women to wear the Hijab in Professional Basketball and as the 2015 Words First Leeds winner which is a National poetry competition partnered by BBC Radio 1Xtra and the Roundhouse.

Asma has been featured on major media outlets such as Vogue Arabia, Cosmopolitan, Hello Magazine, BBC Sport, BBC Three, BBC iPlayer, AJ+, Aljazeera, S24, Channel 4, Buzzfeed and more.

https://www.asmaelbadawi.com/
@asmaelbadawi

# Asma Elbadawi
## Belongings

VERVE
POETRY PRESS
BIRMINGHAM

PUBLISHED BY VERVE POETRY PRESS
https://vervepoetrypress.com
mail@vervepoetrypress.com

All rights reserved
© 2021 Asma Elbadawi

The right of Asma Elbadawi to be identified as author of this work has been asserted in accordance with section 77 of the Copyright, Designs and Patents Act 1988.

No part of this work may be reproduced, stored or transmitted in any form or by any means, graphic, electronic, recorded or mechanical, without the prior written permission of the publisher.

FIRST PUBLISHED FEB 2021

Printed and bound in the UK
by ImprintDigital, Exeter

ISBN: 978-1-912565-50-4

Cover image: Belal Abdelrahman @bash.249

*To my dear mother, father and brother*

# CONTENTS

Introduction

| | |
|---|---|
| Belongings | 13 |
| Headliner | 15 |
| Notes | 16 |
| Banshee | 18 |
| Kandaka | 19 |
| FIBA | 20 |
| Master | 21 |
| Foreign Tongue | 22 |
| Sacrifice | 24 |
| Summer | 25 |
| Prodigal Sun | 27 |
| Soil | 29 |
| Sudan Split | 31 |
| Blade | 33 |
| Playground | 34 |
| Dark & Lovely | 35 |
| Cold | 37 |
| Boys Will Be Boys | 38 |
| Body Language | 40 |
| Broken | 41 |

| | |
|---|---:|
| Baba's Tears | 42 |
| Fireplace | 44 |
| Shades | 46 |
| Entities | 49 |
| Dawn | 50 |
| Cycle of Life | 51 |
| The Waiting Room | 52 |
| Traffic Lights | 55 |
| Lockdown | 56 |
| Parts of Me | 57 |
| Sword | 58 |
| Stake | 59 |
| Half | 61 |
| Cage | 63 |
| Her Story | 64 |
| Handouts | 66 |
| Witness | 68 |
| Praise | 70 |
| Balance | 71 |
| Beloved Pilgrim | 72 |
| Honour | 73 |
| Paradox | 74 |
| Words | 76 |

Acknowledgements

# INTRODUCTION

I found myself writing poetry in private, after a creative writing lesson with Mr Heaton, my year 3 primary school teacher. There was something about it not having to be structured in a particular way that resonated with my young imaginative mind.

By the time I had gone to secondary school, it became a practice I needed to do more often - to organise my thoughts, and make sense of the world around me. I was in constant battles with my teachers. Many of them wanted me to be someone I wasn't. I was far more interested in the arts and sport than all the other subjects they wanted me to give more attention to.

After school, I'd watch def poetry jam. Seeing brave women and men perform spoken word poetry about social issues so eloquently allowed me to experience the power of words. And somewhere at the back of my mind I was inspired to want to do the same one day.

When poetry kept accompanying my images during my studies, I knew my next step was to explore words alone, in front of an audience. So that's what I did. At the start my hands and voice shook, I'd forget my lines and feel so embarrassed but as time went by my confidence grew and the stage became one of my favorite places.

After my performances, hearing my audience's feedback about how they could relate to my work, I always felt thankful and grateful for the journey that had brought me here. And recalled a time when my writing always had red markings on it, pointing out spelling and grammatical mistakes. I remember hearing how my English teacher thought I would fail my English and Literature exams. And how many other teachers predicted I would fail in life too.

This book is proof to me that I didn't fail and a reminder that we are all created in our unique ways, with our own paths and interests and identities. By not conforming to what was expected of me, following my passions and trusting God would lead the way, I found a voice in words I couldn't spell.

I decided to name this book *Belongings*, after the first poem in the collection, in honour of my father who kept encouraging me to use my talents for the greater good, and has stood beside me from the day he walked me to my first day of nursery to standing beside me at my last graduation. And to my mother I dedicate my poem 'Honour', for taking me back to my roots every summer and instilling within me the understanding that faith is the foundation on which everything is built, staying connected to family is important and for teaching me a woman can be both feminine and strong.

The collection itself is a combination of my experiences and the experiences of those who have shared parts of themselves with me. It aims to take the reader on a journey and shed light on the many different personal and social issues we find in society today, covering topics such as mental health, racism, belonging and love.

Traditionally in my Sudanese culture a woman gives away her belongings before marriage. In my case I will be giving away my thoughts. I hope that by sharing them with you, it will give those of you who also write the courage to share your work too. It is by sharing our truths that we can truly understand one another and work towards a more inclusive and diverse world.

Thank you for choosing to accept my belongings, and welcome.

Asma Elbadawi, Sep 2020

# Belongings

# Belongings

Before I am stripped of my belongings and have no tangible hold
on the memories I harvested
There is much to do
There will be a time when I will have to answer to a man
that is not my father and he may not be as understanding
Because he wasn't there the first day of nursery as I stood at the
lanky school gates in my pink dungarees
Nor was he there the day I confessed that maths is one of
my weaknesses
And though I admire the accurate craft of an architect
My hands were not created to build soaring skyscrapers and houses
therefore I am changing my degree
He wasn't there to know that the only sibling I have is a brother and
therefore I understand more about toy hot wheel cars and bb guns
than I do of Barbie and Ken

He may never understand
He may never understand
He may never understand
That my whole life I've worked towards becoming the woman
I am today
The clothes I give away
Have the remanence of my life sewn in them
The watches I wear
Tick between the chapters of my adolescence
The bags I carry
Bear me from one country to another

The name I give away is the name that was used to register me everyday at school
The very same name on my passport and birth certificate

How is it that we erase the history of a woman
As if nothing mattered before her wedding day
Sisters and daughters become wives and mothers
With heavy hearts we are made to say farewell to our former selves.

# Headliner

They won't give me a platform to speak on
Females don't headline nor sell out halls
I'm a woman
Giving me an audience to share my views with would be
a mistake
I'd address issues of race, violence and challenge
the perception of gender roles
I'd tell stories unheard and unspoken
Of how I dared to go offside
How I escaped the kitchen
And travelled far and wide
How my vision never ends
Eyes that have been exposed to darkness and light
How my soul has been ignited by human beings of every kind
How books have expanded my imagination
And given life to my life
Still
They won't give me a platform to speak on
Because I'm a woman
With a voice
Thus
Not woman enough
Art, poetry, sport and the dreams I speak of are to be taken
lightly
*Consider them hobbies* they say
They wont give me a platform to speak on
So I will create my own.

# Notes

I used to be a Sudanese woman of few words harbouring many sentences
Scribbling frustrations about expectations on pages just to make sense of them.
I used to be a woman that engaged in long bouts of awkward silences
A woman of many faces
One for every day of the week and one for different places.
Now I'm engaged to my efforts
Married to the goals I wish to obtain.
Because when you hit rock bottom the rules of the game change
You master techniques that comfort the hunger that roasts within you and fills the gaping holes created in your childhood

And when you've reached adolescence
You come to realise that all everyone possesses are these 4 questions
What do you study?
When will you get a job?
When will you buy a car?
When will you buy a house?


Subconsciously asking *when will you buy happiness*
As if all the answers lay with benjamin
The problem is the only benjamin I know is broke
And I'm not the kind to let spare change define me
So I keep writing

Because to me words unfold like notes
Currency

And untangle the knots that keep me from living my truth
Knots composed by my own people
To separate me from life choices I'm entitled to

*Why didn't you study medicine?*
*Our country needed you*

I wasn't created to be a doctor because even my thoughts bleed
My creativity is like an illness
even psychologists see shrinks

I was a Sudanese woman of few words harbouring many sentences
Now I write
Long after the pages blink.

# Banshee

Maybe my dreams weren't clear enough
Maybe I didn't shout them out loud enough
Maybe I didn't make you aware of my values
Maybe I led you to believe that I was ready to settle for less
That mediocrity
Is an option
That I would stand for nothing
And fall for everything
That I would be a slave to a superficial existence
Maybe I forgot to mention
That with every word I write
Every click of my camera button
I bare my soul
And watch it descend into the distance
Ready to be chewed up and spat out by merciless critics
Maybe my cry for freedom
Was too silent to be heard
Too radical to be accepted
Maybe the court wasn't my place of redemption
Maybe my balanced exterior
Camouflaged my burning desire
To be successful
That above everything
Being anything
But me
Would be a tragedy.

# Kandaka

They call us The Queens, Reina, Königin and Kandakas
Derived from earth
Nurturers and carers
We come in all shades
And hair textures
Some of us carefully fold fabrics over our heads
Devine
Independent
And magnificent
We belong to different nations and tribes
Our tongues are accustomed to different spices
And give off unique aromas of language
Are bodies occupy different spaces
We are skateboarders, designers, singers
Poets, athletes, artists and dancers
Life is created within us
We are fighters
We are the revolution
We are the movement
We are sisterhood
In one with the universe
We feel its murmurs
Shed tears of joy and pain
We are sacred
We are women
No woman
No life.

# FIBA

She ties her shoe laces
Fixes her hijab in front of the mirror
Walks out proudly on to the basketball court
A warrior in the making
Mind vs Body
She speaks the universal language of sport
She has known it ever since she learned how to walk
She dribbles the ball slow
Gains speed and makes her way to the basket
She understands what it takes to make it
Hours in the gym shooting
The kind of woman that believes that we were all created for a purpose
The type to join forces and campaign to pave the way for younger generations when faced with obstacles
She keeps going
For the love of the game
And the many lessons it taught her
For the bonds built between borders
She tells her own story
To remind society that we are human
Our faiths, races and religions do not define us
When you set out into the world to make a difference
Look for common ground
Sport lives in all of us.

# Master

When the boxers are ready to learn
The gloves appear
They will teach them everything they need to know about life
They will test and challenge them
One jab
One punch
At a time
They will separate them from their dreams if they don't have what it takes to make them a reality
Heroes are born out of an unwillingness to accept mediocrity
Or give room for insecurities to settle beneath their flesh
They're driven by passion and determination
They seek God first
Then train their mind and body to predict every movement
Disassemble every pattern before it's fully formed
There is sweat, tears, blood and pain
But the aim is simple
*Eliminate the enemy*
When the boxers' minds and bodies align
The ring appears
The lights will dim
And the crowd will chant
It's fight time.

# Foreign Tongue

Nobody asked me if I wanted to leave you
I was torn from the bosom of your lap
For
10 whole years
I don't know why they long for your barren land
They speak of your tales in a foreign tongue
I try to relate
I just can't understand why they shed tears every time their feet hit your sand
The years spent in Britain
Have eroded my mother tongue
I can no longer *kawn a jumla kamla*
Without borrowing words from the English language
See mother spoke of your tenderness
Father spoke of sacrificing you for the sake of Mohammed and I's education
It's been 20 whole years
And I am beginning to notice
The solacing spectrum of emotions felt under my skin every time that I am here
There is a bittersweet reality to my existence
Time spent searching for the cure to my identity crisis in many countries
Brought me back to this barren land
I regurgitate your tales now as if we are one and the same
Pack segments of dust in my suitcase
To take back to the island from which I came
It's lonely there
*Alghurba Hara*

If only you knew how it felt to be torn from the bosom of your loved ones
Everyone's deserting this once thriving country for a better life
Their gaze says *no hope*
To which my only response is
Hope is in the eyes of the beholder
Change comes from within
From knowing who you are and from where you come
We cannot keep investing outside
And allow our country to crumble
The youth is hungry
The TV screens
Advertise escapism through Capitalism
Self-hate is what they're teaching them
Just keep it fair and lovely
Life is better when you're fair and own many possessions
The only thing greener on the other side is the landscape
Fresh cut grass and clean paths
In this barren land is where you will find happiness
Nobody on the other side is going to invest in your home
Because your home simply doesn't exist in them.

# Sacrifice

I saw parts of me in the flute she played
The sun beat at her golden skin
She said it was the place of sacrifice
I was still searching for home
The flute called out to me
Pulled on strings that were dormant
Tears spoke for me
When I was engulfed in the moment
Seen the sky for the first time in all its glory
Stars led the way
When the world was sleeping
I dreamt of always seeing beyond the surface
The universe heard my prayers
Life keeps picking at my scabs when I least expect it
Resurfaces childhood memories
I never really got over the separation
Though I understand my family' sacrifice
Sometimes I place my phone on airplane mode for weeks and sleep
I find a home in the deafening silence.

# Summer

Winter comes and just like every winter before
I long for summer
I have been here for decades
You would think my flesh would have tightened to accommodate the short days
Thickened to fight the pinching cold and the pearl white crumbling snow
But after that last leaf falls every autumn
Winter arrives
And
I long for summer again
The 6 weeks between 2 school years
Two entities
Two mes
Infused with relatives and screaming kids
Relatives I didn't know existed
Until I was between 11 and 12
And I gazed up at him
My small body reaching half way between the top of his head and the sandy ground beneath his shib shib
I confidently called out into the thick night *baba*
I felt the burning of my cheeks as I realise he was not my father
Interrupted by mother's familiar laugh
*Da amic Maki ya Asma, akho abook*
*This is your uncle Maki, Asma, your daddy's brother*
Her words echoed in my mind
Your daddy's brother
Your daddy's brother
Your daddy's brother

And I had never heard the term *brother* used in this way

Brother was Mohammed
The one that referred to me as his little sister
The one I played football with
The one I picked up two of everything because of
The one I observed finish his ice cream before I ate mine
because I didn't want to be the first to finish mine and be tortured
as I watched him savour every last taste of his

And I guess winter only ever comes to remind me of the warmth
of summer
The parts of me that are missing but always adorned
Summer lives in the cracks of my skin
The smile of my grandfather
The cries of a newborn cousin
and the laughter of my sweet Nile.

# Prodigal Sun

And every time I come back
I slot right back in like I never left in the beginning
Like the years never passed
And elders never aged
And time stood still

And in that moment I inhale the sweet memories that I never made during my childhood
Grasp how it feels to belong amongst relatives, cousins and uncles

I watch the fields yield acres of cotton
And young girls blossom into young women
Their feet embroidered with henna patterns
Dance to the beat of young love
And their shoulders draped with colourful thobs
Bop in the way of tradition

I observe boys come into adolescence
Grow in strength
And learn many of life's valuable lessons
They take on responsibilities once the responsibility of their forefathers
Like true kinsmen

Parents glow with the birth of their infants
And vision life through their existence
Babies grow into toddlers
Their words innocent and unpolished

Leak from the spaces between their milk teeth
Leaving the elders in fits of giggles

We share tales deep into the nights
And around dining tables
Reminiscing previously shared pranks and adventures
The bright white moon in the distance
A witness
To our pure, unsuperficial displays of affection

A world I experience for a short time
Holding the value of a lifetime
A world I briefly taste
Then come to realise
Isn't fully mine.

# Soil

Mother says we are the sons and daughters of our motherland

We are to marry from its soils

Too foreign to fit in

We are the children of the ocean

The waves sway us

Between African territories and Europe

Some days we see home in the eyes of our relatives

Others in the rainy summers of England

I don't pick up the phone to call Afaf

Afraid my tears will unsettle her

*Ana omik o ukhtik o sahbatik*

I try to find sisters in friends

But my friends already have sisters

Seek comfort in my bedroom

The more I am here the more the walls draw in closer

Forcing me to pack my bag

Travel from city to city

Hoping to find home under a random bus shelter, or a country road in the suburbs

Airplanes give me comfort

The sky belongs to its creator

*Wa fil Sammi rizgkom wa ma towadoon*

I wonder what Allah has promised me.

# Sudan Split

We first met as children
When far away
I craved the sweet smell of your herbs and spices
For better or worse
I had a strong desire to be in your presence
Your warmth, generosity, kindness and hospitality wooed me
I edged closer and closer to your lean rich body
Then one day
I woke up
Found myself struggling to toggle you back in
You let go of my hand
Cut me deep
Divided me through the middle
Separated my past and present
Took away the hope, replaced it with fear
An unknown future to the dearest of dear
A territorial battle
How will I greet you now?
If I meet you in the near?
Salute you for holding on so long?
Or do I cry a disheartened tear?
Will I lose a side to which I was briefly introduced?
A side only the elders understood?
I walked and walked endlessly on your roads
Your gritty pavements
Now you may put up a sign
Making the loveliest of places out of bounds
You brought me into this world
Together forever was our fate

Now that you can't handle your responsibilities
You're putting your people out as bait.

# Blade

They ask me to choose a stage name
I choose *Blade*
My words are sharp in nature
That's why my poetry isn't for everyone
I have come to realise that my dreams surface in stages
That's the only way to stomach them
My mother tongue is fading
My colonisers' language unpacked and moved in
I ask myself when is it leaving
My lungs are tired of inhaling
The pen keeps me breathing
But the pen is silent while my motherland is bleeding
Snipers on rooftops silencing the cry for freedom
How many more must lose their life in the pursuit of peace
Caught in the crossfire between different levels of evil?
We are the generation of the ocean
Those who spend their lives wondering which side of the water we mostly belong to
Hailing from rich lands whose leaders are so deceitful
Stacking dollars in offshore accounts while doubling, tripling and quadrupling the price of living
Our parents still dreaming about returning to a Sudan they have known to be peaceful
Back when the Dollar and Jinnah were equal
Back when education was free for everyone
They say power belongs to the people
And I salute my people for reclaiming their power.

# Playground

I wonder if you remember
The words you casually let slip off your tongue
In the school playground
When we were just nine years old
Like a viper spitting out venom?

Or the headlock you stationed me in
Like a criminal at a public execution
Kneed me in the stomach over and over
And let the other children hurl abuse?

I wonder if you know how many times I tried to scrub off
the blackness
Fry the frizziness
Tame my nose
How I even went back to Africa
To find home
And couldn't?

I wonder how you could look me in the eyes during recent
encounters
And walk on by?

I wonder if your chest is too heavy with guilt
To greet me
Ask me about the details of my life
Or if you forgot
Anything ever happened?

# Dark & Lovely

We kept it lovely
In a world that projected fair
Straightened out our curls
And bleached
Listened to you mock the size of our lips and hips until they became trendy
Bit the flesh of our tongues to comfort you when our blackness made you uncomfortable
Let you point out how many foreign friends you have
And how in your house no-one sees colour
Watched you take the lead in our conversations
Equate your struggles to our tribulations
Erase our voice and invalidate our pain
It's not the same because no matter how many times you tan
That colour will wash out in the sink
And you will never understand what if feels to elevate beyond your ends without someone reminding you of the colour of your skin
And when the police pull you up you have plenty of room for error
So when you reach into your pockets
Memorials aren't built upon the blood that has been spilled
The system was created to uplift some and maintain their privileges at any cost
8.46 seconds
Another life lost
It took an *I can't breathe*
For the lullaby to end
And wake the world up from its deep sleep
Realise that on every side of the ocean there are black lives with traumas living in them

We don't choose the colour we are born in
But you can choose to share the oxygen that you breath
Validate our pain and do better
And create a future in which all lives really do matter.

# Cold

I like my cold self
A multitude of emotions
Tucked under a red carpet
Despite the elephant in the room
You'll never see me cry ever
I was raised amongst men
So I'd be damned if a tear was to
Shed light on my fragility
Expose my fears
And paint a perfect silhouette of my insecurities
Survival of the fittest got me lifting
So that even when I put on a dress
I see the strength of a man in the mirror
Accepting inferiority nurtures the idea that amongst us there is a superior gender
Shoots the wombs that provide males with sequels
So I consciously place myself 10 steps ahead
I secure emotions deep into my skin like lotion
Fade out and let the affliction sink in till it's no longer visible
I'm cold
And I like my cold self better
A multitude of emotions tucked under thick carpets forever.

# Boys will be boys

*Don't let them strip you of your masculinity*
Their absent fathers said
As if your masculinity could be shaken
Torn up and given back to you in pieces
Society teaches boys from a young age to mask their fragility with toughness
Shames them whenever they display emotional weakness
He held me
Challenged me
To look him in the eyes and tell him what is a man without his pride
The same eyes that have been dry for so long
I can feel the knots in his chest
That tie him
And choke him
And cause his mind to race with endless thoughts deep into the night
A man without his pride is courageous
Knows that he is a man no matter what
It takes the man in man to open up
Forgive those who tried to destroy him
Even before he has created his own path
From boyhood to manhood

He has to break the cycle
Search for the vulnerability within
And let those tears flow
For how long will we force men to feel foreign in their own bodies?

Restricting their self expression to anger
While they haemorrhage on the inside and
Reach for their fists
To remind others they have the upper hand
The upper hand
That knows no mercy
Demands
Hurts
Abuses
Rapes
Destroys
And once the damage is done
We place the blame and shame on women
And claim *boys will be boys*.

# Body Language

Don't dry your eyes boy
Every part of your body speaks it's own language
The hands of time deemed tears feminine
But emotions live in all of us
Like a bullet
They'll glide under your flesh
Looking for an exit point
Like Russian roulette
You place your life on the line
Maybe this time you'll make it
Or maybe your silent cries
Will rattle the trigger
Society said don't cry boy
Be a man
Don't show any weaknesses boy
The streets won't respect you man
Tell the girl you love her boy
And when you done forget her man
Drench your tongue in profanity boy
No one likes a nice man
And when she raises her voice boy
Remind her who's the man
But when you pull the trigger boy
Society will know
It never raised you
To be a man.

# Broken

He wanted
The smell of wet sand after the rain
He wanted the Nile to flow through my veins
The sky to give birth to stars in a small village in the south
He wanted the colors of our flag to beat from the sun
He wanted hope
A place to locate all his fears
And a map to guide him out of the storms his mind creates
He was just looking for home
And he looked for it in all the places outside of him
At first he would settle in
But with time
Like a child who would break his toys when they stopped making him feel good
He would break everything that's around him
He never came to know that home starts and ends in the spaces between his ribs
He let home stick in his throat
Behind his eyes
And sometimes he almost let home out
But what kind of man would he be if he surrendered to his emotions?
What kind of man would he be if he let others see he was broken?
Just like everyone else he was broken
Trying to gather parts of women to make his part of the world feel whole.

# Baba's Tears

You choked on the verses *kulu nafsin*
I was about ten years old
And I recall hearing yours and mother's reassurances on the telephone
Every Eid
That we would be visiting soon.
And mother never stopped buying sale items from C&A
and Debenhams and placing them in a silver coated trunk
*Kulu nafsin*
And over the years one silver coated trunk became two
And Mohammed and I continued playing together the way children do

But that night was different
Mother hid us away in her Omani friend's flat
Whispered
Don't let them play by the house
Then she came for us in the dead of the night
The scents of the visitors still lingering as she tucked us into bed

After school the next day
You led us in prayer
And you choked on the verses
*kulu nafsin*

Recomposed yourself and continued

*Kulu Nafsin thaigatol mowt*

Obliged to be strong for the family
He on his throne had entrusted onto you
*Kulu nafsin thaigatol mowt*

At 11 we arrived with mother's trunks
The ground shook
Ashamed at the fact that it was unable to wait just
another year
Before it swallowed your
nearest and dearest
*Kulu nafsin thaigatol mowt*

And I never understood the power of those tears
Until I became woman
And learned that boys don't shed tears
Boys hide behind a distorted notion of masculinity

And men
Men....forgive
Men like my father, uncles and brother shed tears
unapologetically
Let their eyes speak for them
Human in every essence of the word

Here is where the beauty lies
The collateral damage where
Love, death and time collide.

# Fireplace

Mama sang in the kitchen
In the loving home of her husband and two children
Longing to be reunited with her extended family
Just for another second
*Life is colder in all forms on this side of the ocean* she would say
I don't know if she ever knew I was listening
Listening to her sing songs about her country
Her parents and siblings
She always spoke in a soft manner
*May God be with you my children*
I can't imagine how hard it must have been
To pack for a year
And remain for a lifetime
My poems speak of home
The same way Mama used to sing to her country
Painful with a sweet melody

One Night
Mama and Baba let me scream
Unfazed by what the neighbors would say
Battling with demons
That have settled in my veins
I kept screaming
I tried to throw out their furniture
Maybe they will leave if my flesh feels less homely
But they secured their chairs and beds back onto the floorboards
Carved paintings on my chest walls
Danced on the carpets

My ribs grew to accommodate them
And to shelter them from the winds
Mama asked me if I felt better after a moment of silence
I guess they had vacated
Or was it that my lungs had simply emptied the toxic fumes from their fireplace?

In the quiet of the night I sing songs my mother used to sing in the kitchen
That remind me of a warmer side to life
Where the car radio blasted out verses of the Quran along the long Madani roads
And my mother's siblings embrace me with open arms in the countryside

This side of the world gets cold
A warmth on the other side of the ocean always awaits me
But my feet are firmly anchored into the footprints of Britain.

# Shades

There are some shades to be ashamed of
Shades too colourful to be hung on the walls of museums
Cloths worn incorrectly
You will never see them in galleries
I wonder what Grandmother would say if I asked her what the colonizers did?
I wonder what shade of women she would describe as strong?
I wonder whose hands shook above the desk
And took beneath the table?
Some fine-dine
Others are deemed erasable

It's not victory if only one race survives
I am here to turn the tables

Wombs are what make women
Not the shade of skin that are born out of them
Some shades think other shades need liberating
Some shades step over other shades to make it

But it's only when all shades come together that we'll truly be able to celebrate
There are some bodies that control other bodies

Male gazes
Instructions on billboards on what our bodies should look like
What clothes are acceptable to wear in which season
Check the catalogues
Sex sells in all seasons

Convinced they need what some bodies sell
They consume
To keep up-to-date with a world that creates insecurities
Then feeds them to its people
Made up
To make us wear makeup
Feel foreign in the bodies we were made in
Those who go against the grain are outcast
True freedom is wrapping material over our bodies anyway that pleases us

Only when we have full control our bodies will we truly be able to celebrate.

She said no
He says she didn't say no because she laughed when she said it
Her no was not no enough
She was too shy to say she wanted it
He says
Her skin felt silk smooth
Running against his cheeks
She says he slobbered all over her
Venom spraying onto her lips
He says her hips swayed
Like a salsa dancer under the moonlight
She says
He forced her thighs to separate
He says we felt as one
She says
He was deaf to the tears
Unaware of her screaming

She SAID *NO*
SHE SAID *NO*

Only when our noes are heard as noes will we truly be able to celebrate.

# Entities

I feel ashamed to complain to the creation when my creator
is present
So I sit back in silence
Motionlessly walking towards my dreams and seeing my friends
sprint right past me with passion
Within me live two entities
One of hope, positivity, joy and gentleness
The other full of negativity, self destructive and angry
And they fight their battles in the pit of my mind mercilessly
Hostage in my own body
Lord have mercy on my soul for I can no longer breathe
I am getting buried alive
People like me are not meant to live in this way
Chains limiting our talents
Pushed to the curb as though we don't deserve success on
this earth
I'm weak because I try to be too strong on my own
And I'm strong because I refuse to be weak amongst others
Time is running
With extreme precision
A cyclic cycle
I watch the sickness inside me intensify then subside over and
over again
Until the mirror refuses to look me in the eyes
A voice inside me quietly whispers
*This life is not worth living*
I don't even look the same anymore
The calm after the storm brings with it new life
An *I cannot and will not accept defeat* kind of mentality.

# Dawn

At the strike of dawn is when it begins
My subconscious wages war on my conscious
I witness the fragility of my existence transcending into
an unsettled distance
My mouth stutters
Searches for any one of its mother tongues
*Ana* (I)
can't
*athamal* (take this)
Succumbing to the illusion that I'm not strong enough

Weakness is a state of mind
I mutter under tangled breaths
Weakness is a state of mind
I drag my limbs
Weakness is a state of mind
I pour holy water on an anatomy that keeps betraying me
Weakness is a state of mind
How many more times must I drown myself, to remember how to breathe?
Weakness is a state of mind
I gasp for fresh air
Weakness is a state of mind
I break an oath with my demons
Weakness is a state of mind
I make my way back to the convent
And ignite the conviction in me
That I will never surrender
To a weak state of mind.

# Cycle Of Life

Womanhood came too quick
I never got the chance to say *goodbye girl*

Before my first period dried up
*Hush* society said

They put shame in us
Before we learn to love our own bodies

Every month from then on
I silenced the piercing pain

Withdrew from the world to dance with demons that like to play mind games
And when it ceased to be fun
I stopped feeding them to tighten in their reins

The party always ended when the blood cleared
But the demons never really disappear
They're just waiting for the next cycle to begin.

# The Waiting Room

I don't know why I feel the way I do
Why the future seems so scary
Why my heart races the moment I wake up
And my whole life flashes before me
I can't do this
I really can't do this
I can't face another day, another minute here
Breathe slow
I reassure my racing heart I can do this
I can do this
Sometimes I seek comfort in my bedroom
Watch back to back episodes on Youtube and Netflix
Read a book or two
Order in a takeaway
Sleep then sleep some more
Stacks of plates begin to pile up beside me
Dirty laundry spreads on the floor like a carpet
Vivid dreams
Palpitations
Sweaty palms
Short breaths
Dr said talking about it will help
Until then try out these pills
The only person I am talking to is myself
Agitated
Waiting for my name to make it on top of a waiting list
Tried the pills but was sick of the numbness
Night and day have merged into one

Have I showered?
Maybe yesterday
Maybe not in days
I lost count
I need to escape this

Looking forward to a fresh start
I jot down plans
List friends I can't wait to catch up with
Maybe I will go shopping
Switch up my style
Get my nails done
Buy some new perfume
Find love
Settle down
Have some kids
Who knows
I'm healing and embrace what's to come

Without warning
The novelty wears out
Triggered
I can't do this
I let my mind trick me into a false sense of security
The more I travel
The heavier the baggage gets
The anxiety I left behind keeps following me
Like a thief
Constantly stealing my hopes
Leaving me at the mercy of fear
My ribs tighten
Body assembles

Chooses fight over flight to fight off the danger my mind has presented
I have accepted that help will never come in the form of human contact
I'm screaming *WHY GOD WHY?*
I didn't do anything to deserve this
When will I be free to live my life?
I can't do this
I really can't do this
I drag my suitcase back to my bedroom
Convinced it's my only place of sanctuary
Only to repeat the cycle again
I don't know why I feel the way I do
Why the future seems so scary.

# Traffic Lights

When the heart dries out
The tears stop beating
You collect pieces of yourself
And glue them together with emptiness
Eyes fixed blankly at a future that you had believed in
You question the reason for your existence
Because now you think you're incapable of achieving anything
The dishes have not been made
And the bed has not been washed
Time ticks between your thoughts to awaken your consciousness
Outside the traffic lights are still functioning
Amber
Green
But you're stuck on red.

# Lockdown

Everything feels so surreal right now
Our new norm is social distancing
Disconnecting from connections we have worked so hard
to build over the years
Job redundancies
And uncertainties
Self-isolating in houses some of us never spent enough time
to make homes in
Never wanted to come face to face with loneliness
Never gave our minds time to fixate on could have beens
Should have beens
We are human beings
Brought together by this universal moment in history
That will make or break us
Redefine how we perceive ourselves and one another
Will we succumb
To our survival of the fittest instincts
Or will we unite as one in our bid to fight this?
I hope in the midst of this chaos we can learn to look within
Appreciate the healing power of slowing down
Find alternative ways of living
Where our houses begin to feel like homes
And we make time for the people that matter
And when all this is over
We can come out stronger and more connected
To a healthier world
And more meaningful future.

# Parts of me

It's been months since we last spoke
Months since I last gripped you tightly
Months since I let the ink spill out onto these pages
Life happened so fast I didn't get a chance to address the parts of me that where still hurting
I always found beauty in capturing pain
Then gifting those parts of me to complete strangers
But some wounds take longer to part with
And even when they're at the tip of your tongue
Somehow you find a way to silence them
Shame with a pinch of *no one will understand,* some noes are met with violence
Some noes are heard as yeses
And some yeses are said for the sake of survival
This is the part I'd usually part with, the parts of me that are still hurting
But I'm not ready to gift parts of me to complete strangers.

# Sword

The weight slipped off like a bandage
Revealing the parts of me that haven't recovered
I thought I was past that
Took the past on the chin
And dashed it
Rewrote my life
After you write lies for so long the pen senses
Demands your truth or it stops expressing
The pen was my sword but the pen stopped communicating
The pages stuck within me need to be purged
I'm struggling to get the letters out
Form the words that will reveal sentences concealed beneath my flesh
In the last third of the night I screamed
GOD SEES EVERYTHING
Not sure if it was a cry for revenge or a *HELP ME*
These days I lose consciousness
Letting the weight slip off as a defence mechanism
I can't give in to the hunger
*You will achieve great things if you restrict for longer*
The body I'm in feels foreign
Disgusted
At what I see in the mirror
I should eat
But I can't
I need the control
I'm nursing my wounds
They need to be purged
*God sees everything.*

# Stake

It's just you and I
Dining
And no matter how hard I try to digest you, I just can't
My bones are starting to scratch beneath the surface of my skin
My mind flickers in the company of others
I count the hours and days since I last engulfed you
There is victory in holding out longer
Long enough for them to hear me silently call out for help
I'm too much of a coward to slit
So I restrict
To drown out the trauma
If I can't control my life
Then hopefully this will help me leave sooner
Or at least ward off their glances
Ever since that first drop of blood
My body has belonged to the consumers
Billboards
Music videos
And Ads
With perfect Abs
Gaps between thighs
And bubble butts
Every season brings with it a new trend
Are you a contender?
Do you have what it takes to keep changing with the times and get the man willing to bid the highest price to purchase a commodity?
Or do you want to remain
Disposable

And replaceable?
So you keep up
Girl you keep up with every trend
Take on every fad diet and exit every piece of fat from beneath your skin
Cut your hair
Die it
Relax it
Extend it
Bleach your skin
Tan it
Nip and tuck away at your every imperfection
Question your beauty in every mirror reflection
Wonder if you're enough
If anyone will ever like you
Anyone will ever marry you
So I dine with you
But I can't eat you
There is too much at stake.

# Half

I share half
Half because the other half can't be stomached
People will put you on pedestals and then pull the rug from beneath you when your voice unsettles them
I build my life on being unsettled
Not quite belonging to here nor there
Fighting a mind that paces between *I can do anything*
And *I don't wanna be here*
Some days I'm here to eat
I bring the full table to the table
It's a family feast
Some days I'm silent
Not ready to say the things the world wants me to say
So I speak in whispers
Loud enough for my creator to hear me struggle
Silent enough to be forgotten by the creation
Not all voices were made to be seen on your phone screen
Some voices shake when they address strangers
Some sing praises to their creator on a moonlit Summer night
Some cry to their lord to ease the grief
Some murmur behind thick curtains on cold Winter's eves
All voices reach their destinations and serve their purpose one way or another
Reunite families after years of feud
Start revolutions
Settle an unsettled infant
Console a friend
Show a grandparent that they're loved

Let a mother and father know that they're cherished
Not all voices are made to be seen
I share half with the world
And leave the other half unseen.

# Cage

In many ways I trapped her
Kept her away from the world incase they hurt her
When no one was around
I let her out for a while
Then without warning I hid her
As time went by I started to overfeed her
I sensed her grow inside of me
Until my body could no longer contain her
She spread her wings
And broke out of the cage in which I imprisoned her
Now she accompanies me wherever I go
She protects me from the world
I no longer protect her
She is the most beautiful part of me
Her name is Joy.

# Her Story

I couldn't see beyond the figures she listed
15 dead 117 injured
My inability to process her pain kept me heartless
I am 1
My mind incapable of comprehending the struggle of an entire nation
My eyes have gotten used to the images of missiles and nameless dead babies
Everything about her lifelong battle was alien to me
Besides
This war is not on my front door
So I shall remain silent

She could not see beyond the gimmicks I sold
Her inability to comprehend that I show no resemblance to the materialistic world I live in
Kept her bitter
She believed I couldn't possibly have problems of my own
Because unlike her I live in the west and possess a freedom
of expression
She couldn't understand why I didn't use this to my advantage
Why my statuses had no remnants of the distaste for the war that has settled at her front door
Why like the rest of the world I choose to press mute on her news and remain silent

Then one day as we conversed
She felt the sadness behind my laughter
Posed the question

*Why are you happy yet sad?*
I caught a glimpse of the invisible vessel that connected us
As she continued
*I am human just like you, I have bad and good days, I am both strong and weak*
And from that moment on
We made it our mission to sing each other's song
And be the back to each other's bone.

With unity comes strength
And only then
Can we break the silence.

# Handouts

She stands in line
Reduced to 1 of the hundreds whose
ID cards are called out in the backyards of community centres
Hands reach out for a sack of rice, pasta and handouts
At the back of her mind she wonders whether the children have been orphaned or is the father still alive?
Still missing
It's been 5 years,
Still missing
7 months
Still missing
19 days
Still missing
20
21
She hasn't stopped counting
The relatives advise it's time to move on
But how does a wife bury a husband that has
not yet been pronounced.........?


She sits at home
Afraid of a world that may never see her children grow
Eyes filled with tears
Her mind knows that souls belong to their creator and he returns them as and when he pleases
Her heart pleads with him to keep them for as long as she is breathing
Long enough for her to see them in their graduation robes

Long enough for her to dance at their weddings
Long enough to see her grandchildren playing

He never gave up
Never stopped dreaming of returning to his home
Where the soil is fertile
Where he knows how to sew seeds to make an honest living
Shrapnel in his leg
Forced him to get it amputated
His shame is his inability to provide for his family
In a country whose land will never feel like home

A 3 year old boy stopped talking
Petrified of what would pour out of his lips if he allowed them to expose his memories
He was born in a country where the sky calls out to its people
Inviting them to death
A people whose only chance to survive is to escape everything they have ever known
Only to be washed out on beaches
Hidden in open air prisons
Tucked away in inner cities so no one will see them

Refugees
The people whom war came to by surprise
Separated generations
Destroyed homes
Livelihoods
And dreams.

# Witness

Her name was Witness
Born to a father and mother
Who encouraged her to always pursue her dreams
She joined the other children as they picked berries and climbed trees

She woke up one morning to find her favorite trousers wouldn't stretch over her hips
She couldn't get her head around why a single hair appeared on her armpit

Then one day she saw it
The little murky stain
That indicates that she was now an object
Her body no longer hers
And open to judgment
She peered into emptiness
No tear, no cry
She hid the evidence
Vowed to never tell a soul of today's incident
She understood far too well its consequences

The stabbing pain betrayed her
Mother said she shouldn't play outside any more
She should wear longer clothes
And look to the ground when she walks
It's not that she didn't trust her
But we live in a world
Where men are vultures

School became different
Her teacher lingered
Asked for favours she didn't want to offer
Every *no* was a beating or even worse a failed exam paper
He told her
*Look, your future is in my hands*
*And you'll enjoy it once you experience the pleasure*
Fearing for what could become of her if she didn't submit
to his wishes
She gave in
It became a daily ritual

The shame silenced her
She took off
Before it was obvious that she harboured life within her
Resorted to cooking and housekeeping in a home in a city far
from where she was raised
To provide herself with shelter
She kept her gaze to the ground
And blended in with the furniture

At night she would look at the child she bore
Sickened at her inability to love her daughter the way her mother
had loved her
Half of her was half of him
And she couldn't forgive him for the life he stole from her
Feeling alone
She longed for the days of innocence
Back when her favorite trousers fit perfectly over her hips
And she picked berries and climbed trees with the other kids.

# Praise

In a different realm
My soul accepted the responsibility of trust
An honor the heavens and mountains could not bare
Like every test
The soul must face obstacles
Challenges that make it question its strength
My soul lost direction
Turned from *ahdina alsirat al mustageem*
To validate its existence
In tune with iTunes
Body dances
*Keke* do you love me?
Body spots its imperfections
Body mirrors bodies on screens
To find its happiness
Body is empty
Body works hard to succeed in a 9-5 regime
Body is empty
Body frantically searches for acceptance in the hearts of others
Body is empty
Body searches for soul
But soul has never been nourished
Only a soul fed *thikr* is a soul replenished
*Subhan Allah walhamdulillah wa la lillahi Ila Allah wallahu akbar.*

# Balance

I keep losing my balance
In a world I long to leave a legacy in on my departure
Wondering why it's so difficult to seal my closeness with you
Why it's forever fluctuating
Between
I feel you in the cracks of my skin
The air that I breathe
To searching for you in every aspect of my life
Struggling to keep your closeness even when you're closer to me than my own jugular vein
I flick through pages of verses in my pursuit of self-healing
Learning that I can't do it on my own
*I am close to answer the call of the caller if he calls*
So I call
With arms wide open
Pleading with you
*Do not entrust me to myself even for the blink of an eye*
For every ground I try to build foundations on other than you proves unstable
Every soul I rest on
Doesn't catch me every time I fall
Every rib I build a shelter in
Isn't safe enough for me to call home
*You are the everlasting*
There is no balance without you
So I will keep toiling towards you in my state of imbalance until I meet you.

# Beloved Pilgrim

Oh beloved
Send my peace and blessings to the beloved
Every year I have felt disconnected from the journey of the pilgrims
Who set sail over land, sea and sky to reach our *Habeeb Almustafa*
But this year you carry part of me with you and I feel his presence
Hear him return my *sallam*
Sense my heart soften
I have spent my youth wavering
Trying to find meaning to life
With every footstep you take
I long to be invited to stand side by side with the men and women
Who will return from their Lord's home
Sinless and pure like the day their mothers gave birth to them

*"Allah and His Angels send blessings on the Prophet, O you who believe!
Send your blessings on him, and salute him a thorough salutation"*

# Honour

We met when I was born
To her I was the companion she was waiting for
She dreamt about me ever since she came of age
And knew she could have children of her own
How I would look
How she would dress me
So many things she couldn't wait to teach me
She knew I would be one of a kind
Unique in every way
Because I was created from her
For her
And I will never forget how
She held me and my brother's little hands
As we walked to school
Reciting verses of the Quran
*Gul huwa Allahu ahad*
She lay the most beautiful foundation in life for us
Islam
And even when I strayed
I came back because she had given me the sweet taste of Iman
And as they say
Whoever tastes the sweetness of Iman will always recognise the bitterness of sin
She is my lifelong companion
My next of kin
And as I'm growing older
Physically I am starting to look like my mother
Now I wonder was I created for her or was she created for me?
Either way I wear her features like a badge of honour.

# Paradox

Time is teaching me maybe I wasn't built to build
My emotions run too deep to keep building on my own
I find myself biting my tongue a little harder
Locking the words *I miss you* between my jaws
Refusing to acknowledge the pain of separation
That I experience every time he is not near
How weak will I seem?
Admitting that my body is accustomed to missing
Yet yearns to settle in the space between his ribs
And my way of living is so fiercely Alpha female
That I'm battling the urge to drop the amour that has shielded me
for years and give in to him to lead & protect


Or maybe my resistance comes from knowing all my parts
The ones I face but can't let others come face to face with
Like the days when sleeping soothes sensations too heavy to bear
And the walls keep caging in
Forcing me to pack and run home to my home away from home
across the border
Or when food gets stuck in my throat
And every part of me wants to choke me for not being stronger


Or maybe love is too raw
Too chaotic to be tamed
Too sacred and pure
Too much for some
Just right for those brave enough to face their own fears
and let love in

I'm just a paradox
Too strong to let anyone in
Too human to do it on my own.

# Words

Someone once told me
You should fear writers
They will dissect your wounds
And present you with them as words
Sentences
Sharp enough to pierce right through you
Let you question
At what point did you drop your armour long enough for them?
To read all your fears
Watch you grapple with your mind
Wonder if you're strong enough to lay with your nightmares
And come out of the other end gasping for air
Use whatever remaining breaths you have left to drag your limbs to safe haven
Bathe in your dreams
And make them a reality
Or if you will choke

The same person once told me
That you should never trust a poet
They have the ability
To spin silk-smooth words that will leave you enchanted
Believing everything they tell you
Holding on to every thread
Drop your armour
Pied pipers, you will find yourself dancing to their sweet tunes
Follow them into whatever danger zone they planted
Fall deeply
For them to leave you hanging

No one stopped to ask how do writers and poets translate raw emotions so eloquently?
What whirl-wind of a storm must their life be in to feel so deeply?

Luckily someone once told me that there is power in your words
People will always fear people like you
Never lose your voice
Use it even if it's shaking.

ACKNOWLEDGEMENTS

Here is where I say thank you to everyone who has been part of my journey thus far; the mentors, professors and teachers who have believed in me; my friends who have embraced, comforted and encouraged me to write my truth; the beautiful individuals I have met over the years who have shared parts of them with me and allowed me to weave their stories into words; my parents and brother who have loved and supported me throughout my life and accepted me as I am. A special thank-you to Mr Heaton, my Year 3 primary teacher, for teaching me how to write poetry and to God for answering my prayers and giving me this gift to share with the world.

Thank you to you all and may peace be with you.

## ABOUT VERVE POETRY PRESS

**Verve Poetry Press** is a quite new and already award-winning press that focused initially on meeting a local need in Birmingham - a need for the vibrant poetry scene here in Brum to find a way to present itself to the poetry world via publication. Co-founded by Stuart Bartholomew and Amerah Saleh, it now publishes poets from all corners of the UK - poets that speak to the city's varied and energetic qualities and will contribute to its many poetic stories.

Added to this is a colourful pamphlet series, many featuring poets who have performed at our sister festival - and a poetry show series which captures the magic of longer poetry performance pieces by festival alumni such as Polarbear, Matt Abbott and Geraldine Carver.

Like the festival, we strive to think about poetry in inclusive ways and embrace the multiplicity of approaches towards this glorious art.

In 2019 the press was voted Most Innovative Publisher at the Saboteur Awards, and won the Publisher's Award for Poetry Pamphlets at the Michael Marks Awards.

www.vervepoetrypress.com
@VervePoetryPres
mail@vervepoetrypress.com